Come to Jesus

Newman Hall

Bibliographic Information

Christopher Newman Hall (1816 – 1902), one of the most celebrated English Nonconformist divines of the nineteenth century and personal friend to C. H. Spurgeon, published the gospel tract, *Come to Jesus* in 1848. By the end of the century, it was republished into forty different languages and had sold in excess of four million copies worldwide. This reprint edition reflects the 1863 publication by the Evangelical Tract Society in Petersburg, Virginia.

an Ichthus Publication edition

Copyright © 2014 Ichthus Publications
ISBN 10: 1502766906
ISBN 13: 978-1502766908

www.ichthuspublications.com

CONTENTS

Preface 5

Come to Jesus 7

Why Should I Come?

You Are A Sinner, Come for Pardon 8

God is Angry—Come to be Reconciled 9

Hell Awaits You—Come to be Saved 10

For Peace of Conscience, Come 12

For A New Heart—Come 13

For the Privileges and Joys of Adoption—Come 14

That You May Enter Heaven—Come 16

Who Is Jesus?

Jesus Is God 17

Jesus Is Man 18

He Is the Saviour of Sinners 20

He Is the Only Saviour 21

He Is A Loving Saviour 22

He Will Be Our Judge 24

Where Is Jesus? 25

What Is Meant by "Coming to Jesus?" 26

Come by Prayer 28

Come In the Boldness of Prayer 29

Come In Faith 30

Come As A Sinner—Just As You Are 31

"But I Am Not Worthy, and Cannot Come Aright." 33

"But I Fear I Am Not One of the Elect." 34

"But I Have No Faith." 35

Ye Who Are Young, Come 37

Ye Who Are Advancing In Years, and Ye Who Are Aged, Come 38

Backslider, Come 39

Despairing Sinner, Come 41

Careless Sinner, Come 42

Come Now: It Will Be Harder Work Tomorrow 43

Come Now: Tomorrow May Be Too Late 45

You Must Perish If You Do Not Come 46

PREFACE

LISTEN, DEAR FELLOW-SINNER. How kind, how wonderful an invitation is this! God speaks, and speaks to THEE. The Father says, "COME." The Son says, "COME." The Holy Spirit says, "COME." The blessed angels echo the cry, "COME." Many poor sinners who have accepted the call, join their voices in the appeal, and say, "Come to Jesus." This little book unites in the entreaty, poor sinner, and with all earnestness, plainness and affection, implores thee to "COME TO JESUS."

When he was himself on earth, well knowing and full of pity for the sufferings and sins of men, as he looked round on the crowd which one day surrounded him, he tenderly said,

> "Come unto me, all ye that labor and are heavy laden, and I will give you rest" (Matt. 11:28-30).

What he said then he says NOW. The invitation he gave to the men of that day, he gives to THEE, my fellow-sinner: "Come unto me." Art thou not heavy laden with guilt? O then come to Jesus and thou shalt find rest. COME TO JESUS; COME TO JESUS.

COME TO JESUS

HE PROMISES REST. BUT far better than rest of body is rest of soul. It is wretched to be a slave, to groan, bleed, toil; but far worse to be Satan's bondman, dragging about an evil conscience and an aching heart. Rest from this cannot be had but by coming to Jesus. And if we come, he will lighten every other load. Are you poor? Come, and he will make you rich for ever. Are you sick? Come, and he will cure your worst disease. Are you sad? Come, and he will wipe away your tears. Are you bereaved? Come, and he will be to you a brother in adversity, who changes not, and never dies. Is sin a burden? O then come to Jesus and he will take it all away. Do you dread the day of death and judgment? Come, and that day will be the dawn of life and glory. O then come. To be merely called by such a person should be enough to make us glad. Of a stranger, we might say, "Perhaps he intends me no good;" of a poor man, "He cannot assist me, however willing;" of a selfish rich man, "Who can expect aught from him?" But if a Howard or a Wilberforce said to a mourner, "Come," he might feel quite sure some kindness was intended. Now he who invites thee, sinner, is both able and willing to help. He has clothes for the naked, food for the hungry, wealth for the poor, eternal life for all. His very word, "Come," is enough to make thee glad. A blind beggar by the way side, hearing he was passing, cried out, "Mercy, mercy!" The people told him to be quiet; but he shouted the louder, "Have mercy on me!" Jesus invited him: and then some said, as though he might now be quite sure of a blessing, "Be of good comfort; rise, he calleth thee." They knew Jesus never called and then refused; and so they told him to rejoice. Sinner, be you of good cheer; the, same Jesus calleth thee. As the blind man threw off his cloak lest it should hinder him, do you cast off every sin that would stop you—rush through every crowd of difficulties, and falling at the feet of Jesus say, "Have mercy on me? I am blind, I am lost; save, or I perish." Are you too great a sinner? The more need to come. Have you a guilty conscience? With that guilty conscience come. Have you a wicked heart? With that wicked heart come. Have you nothing with which to purchase his favor? "Without money" come. Rich and poor, masters and servants, old and young, white man and black, sinners, of every class, COME.

∽ ∾

Why Should I Come?
You Are A Sinner, Come for Pardon

PERHAPS YOU DO NOT FEEL you are a sinner. At least, you think you are no worse than others, but better than many. You are no drunkard, thief, adulterer, but keep the Sabbath, read the Bible, and attend the house of God. But have you indeed obeyed all the commandments? Never broken any of them? Always been true, chaste, sober, honest, forgiving, kind? Never indulged in pride, malice, anger, deceit, or lust? God requires purity of heart as well as of outward conduct, and he knows all our thoughts. Have you then never cherished the thought of sin in your heart, though you have feared outwardly to commit it? Besides, the first and chief command is, to love the Lord our God with all our mind and strength. Have you always done this; always been thankful for his mercies; always carefully read his word in order to obey it; always tried to please him, loved to pray to him, taken delight in his day, his people, his worship; always striven to be "holy as he is holy," to make known his truth, to induce others to love him, and endeavored in all things to glorify him? If you have always done this, you have still only just done your duty, and have nothing to boast of. But you have not done it. Conscience tells you so. You know you have sinned thousands of times. You know you have sought your own pleasure, and in your best actions you have not been prompted by a desire to please God. You have lived for yourself; you have sought man's approval, but God has not been in all your thoughts. The Bible tells us,

> "If man say he hath no sin, he deceiveth himself. There is none righteous, no, not one. All have sinned, and come short of the glory of God."

O, my fellow-sinner, is it not true of thee, "The God in whose hand thy breath is, and whose are all thy ways, thou hast not glorified?" You are a sinner. Guilt, enormous guilt hangs upon you. In God's book all your sins are written down. You cannot get rid of them. Were you to labour for thousands of years, you could not atone for the least. All you could do would only be your duty. Paying today's debt still leaves yesterday's where it was. And were you to give all you possess, or suffer torture and death, it would not take away sin. The past cannot be recalled. But there is forgiveness, free, full, eternal, for the guilty. Jesus has pardon for thee, sinner, purchased with his own blood. Come for it. Come to Jesus Christ for it.

God is Angry—Come to be Reconciled

THE BIBLE SAYS "GOD is angry with the wicked every day. He hateth all workers of iniquity." And has not God much cause to be angry with thee, sinner? He gave and preserves your life and faculties, and bestows all your comforts. Yet you forget him. He has told you his commands; and these are all intended to do you good, yet you do not regard them. You do not reverence God, but live almost as if there was no such Being. What an ungrateful son would you be, if thus you treated your parents—if you avoided their company, disliked to think of them, and disregarded their wishes! Hear then what God says:

> "Hear, O heavens, and be astonished, O earth! I have nourished and brought up children, and they have rebelled against me."

He is full of love to you, as a tender Father; but by your sins you have grieved him. Besides, he is your Creator, King, and righteous Judge, and must and will punish all sinners. He must act, to those who rebel, not as a kind parent, but as an angry monarch. It is your own fault, however, that he is angry. You make him so. Your sins separate between you and God. As long as you live without repenting of sin, his anger must ever be hot against you, sinner, and you cannot escape or hide from him. Wherever you are, he is there, and he is angry. He "compasses your path and your lying down," and he is angry. It depends on him whether or not you draw your very next breath, and he is angry. O sinner, better for all the world to be angry with thee than God. What an awful life is yours! The "wrath of God abideth on you." How dreadful to feel when going to bed, "God is angry"—to awake and know "God is angry,"—wherever you go, and whatever you do, "God is angry." And O, to die knowing that "God is angry;" and to stand before his judgment seat, and see that he is angry. Sinner, he is angry only while you make him so; he is willing to be your friend; he sent his Son with this message, "Be ye reconciled to God." If you will give your heart to that Messenger, and trust in him, all this anger will cease. O then, come to Jesus. Be no longer Gods foe, but accept the offer be his friend. But beware, beware of rejecting Jesus; for he says, "He that believeth not," that is, does not come to "the Son, shall not see life, but the wrath of God abideth on him."

Hell Awaits You—Come to be Saved

HELL IS NOT A FABLE invented by priests to frighten their fellow-men; but as sure as the Bible is the word of God, so sure is it that "the wicked shall be turned into hell, and all nations that forget God." "It is appointed unto men once to die, but after this the judgment." "Then all men must give an account of the deeds done in the body." "God will judge the secrets of men." Then all sinners who have not obtained pardon by coming to Jesus will be on the left hand of the Judge, who will pronounce their dreadful sentence, "Depart, ye cursed into everlasting fire, prepared for the devil and his angels." O who can tell the torments of that place? No more pleasant light of day, no more cheerful voice of friends, no more comforts of home, no more pleasures of the world and sin. The rich man can take none of his wealth with him, the gay man none of his amusements. Conscience will dart its sting past sins will be clearly remembered, and past opportunities of escape now gone for ever. O, that one of them might come back! O for one more Sabbath! O for one more hour to pray for mercy! But it will be then too late, too late. Darkness for ever, sin for ever, woe for ever, death for ever. Jesus speaks of it as,

> "the lake that burneth with fire and brimstone—outer darkness, where there is weeping and wailing and gnashing of teeth—where the worm dieth not, and the fire is not quenched"—

where the wicked rich man, being in torments, cried out,

> "Send Lazarus, that he may dip the tip of his finger in water, and cool my tongue, for I am tormented in this flame."

There he that is filthy shall be "filthy still," and "the smoke of their torment ascendeth up for ever and ever." What misery can be greater than what such words as these describe? How dreadful, then, to be in hell! What more horrible? And every unforgiven sinner is on his way to it. You whose eye now reads this page, if you are not pardoned, you are on your way. Every hour brings you nearer. Once there, and all hope is gone for ever. But is there no escape? Yes; one way, and one only. Flee to Jesus. He came to save from hell. "God so loved the world that he gave his only begotten son that whosoever believeth in," cometh to, "him, should not perish, but have everlasting life."

Nothing can save you if you will not come; nothing can prevent your salvation, if you do come.

∽ ∾

For Peace of Conscience, Come

"THERE IS NO PEACE, saith my God, to the wicked." Some sinners seem to be at peace, but it is only by refusing to think. They will not consider. But such thoughtlessness is not worthy to be called peace. It is like a man in a sinking ship, who will not examine what is the danger; or like a tradesman, who fancies all is not going on well, but will not look into his accounts, lest his mind should be disturbed. So the sinner fancies something is wrong, and fearing to be made unhappy, he banishes reflection about God and his soul. Yet every sinner thinks sometimes, and then he must be wretched. When death visits a neighbors house, or enters his own, or threatens himself, and at many other times, the thought will come, "God is angry; my soul is in danger; I am not fit to die." And how much such a thought damp his pleasure, and disturb his repose.

No, you cannot be at peace till you have obtained pardon. You may try all the pleasures of the world in turn, you may seek to drown thought by plunging deeper and deeper into sin, but you cannot be happy. But when we come to Jesus, all our sins a e at once forgiven. We still think of them with sorrow, but we need no more think of them with terror. God says to us, "Your sins and your iniquities will I remember no more." He blots out "all trespasses." He "casts them behind his back into the depths of the sea." They will not be mentioned at the judgment day. "He will abundantly pardon." He now regards us with love. We need not be afraid of him. He invites us to trust him as a kind friend. Instead of hiding from him, as Adam did, we may hide in him, as David did, saying, "Thou art my hiding place." O what a happy change! I am a sinner still, but a sinner pardoned, reconciled, saved. And whatever dreadful things conscience may tell me, Jesus says, "Thy sins are forgiven thee; go in peace." "Peace I leave with you, my peace I give unto you." "Being justified by faith, we have peace with God through our Lord Jesus Christ." Poor sinner, you and peace have long been strangers. Worldly pleasure is not peace; and nothing can give it while you and God are enemies, and your sins hang heavily on your soul. Come then to Jesus. He both makes and gives peace. Seek pardon through him, and you will soon know what is meant by "the peace of God which passeth all understanding."

❧ ☙

For A New Heart—Come

"YE MUST BE BORN AGAIN," said Christ to Nicodemus. There must be a great change in our thoughts and feelings respecting God, before we are able to serve him on earth and enjoy him in heaven. Sin has estranged our minds from God, so that we do not desire him and love him. True religion is not pleasant to us. This is being "carnally minded, which is death." To love the things which sin makes distasteful is a great change, like coming to life. It is called the new birth, or regeneration. "Verily, verily I say unto thee, Except a man be born again, he cannot see the kingdom of God." Unconverted sinner, how can you expect to enter heaven? You would not be happy there. A swallow enjoys the air, and a cow the meadows, but a fish would soon languish there and die; there must be adaptation. Music charms those alone who have an ear for it; books are no treat to those who dislike reading; and society is only pleasant when it is congenial. A clown would not feel at ease at court, the ignorant cannot enjoy the company of the learned, the profligate do not love the society of the virtuous; and just so the ungodly cannot take pleasure in religion. Is not the Sabbath to you a dull day, the Bible a dry book, religious conversation unpleasant, prayer a task, and the company of the pious irksome? But heaven is all Sabbath, all worship, all holiness—its inhabitants all righteous; and their talk and actions all have reference to God. Heaven is happy because it is holy, and because God is there. But if you do not love holiness and God, it would not be a happy place for you. You would wander about a miserable, solitary thing, damping the enjoyment you could not share, and polluting the temple in which you alone would be made to worship.

Therefore, unless born again, you never will enter. You cannot, I know, change your own heart, but the Spirit of God can. And Jesus died to obtain for us the gift of the Spirit. And this gift is freely bestowed on all who sincerely apply to the Saviour for it. O then earnestly pray for the Spirit of God, that you may be born again. Come to Jesus with the petition of David, "Create in me a new heart, O God, and renew a right spirit within me." And for your encouragement, think of the gracious assurance of Christ,

> "If ye, being evil, know how to give good gifts unto your children, how much more shall your Father, which is in heaven, give the Holy Spirit to them that ask him?"

For the Privileges and Joys of Adoption—Come

PERSONS OF WEALTH SOMETIMES take the children of the poor, and train them as their own; this is called adoption. And thus God describes his treatment of those who come to Jesus. "Ye shall be my sons and daughters, saith the Lord God Almighty." "We have received the Spirit of adoption, whereby we cry, *Abba*, Father." We are permitted, in prayer, to address God as "our Father, which art in heaven." He loves these adopted children with more than an earthly parent's affection. He teaches, watches over, comforts, feeds, protects them. Sorrows are his kind chastisements, intended for their benefit.

> "If ye endure chastening, God dealeth with you as with sons; for whom the Lord loveth, he chasteneth."

In all their trials, he consoles them.

> "Like as a father pitieth his children, so the Lord pitieth them that fear him."

> "As one whom his mother comforteth, so will I comfort you."

Sickness, poverty, bereavement, all their troubles, are overruled for their advantage. "All things work together for good to them that love God." "They shall not want any good thing." "No weapon formed against them shall prosper." In every difficulty and danger their Father is at their side.

> "Fear not; for I have redeemed thee. I have called thee by thy name; thou art mine. When thou passest through the waters, I will be with thee; and through the rivers, they shall not overflow thee."

"I will never leave thee nor forsake thee." They may tell their Father all their wants. "In everything make known your requests unto God." His ear is ever open to their cry, and his hand ever outstretched to do them good. As a Father, he provides for them an inheritance; but unlike those of earth, it is "incorruptible, undefiled, and fadeth not away." Oh what happiness to be a child of God; to feel:

> "God is my Father! He loves me, pities, pardons, keeps me. I am safe from all evil. Wicked men and wicked spirits cannot harm me. God is my refuge, ever near; and he never slumbers, never is weary, never forgets, and will never change. He says, 'I have loved thee with an everlasting love.' He will be always near me while on my journey here, and at last will take me to dwell with him in his palace forever."

What earthly greatness can equal this? Reader, would you be a child of God! You may, if you come to Jesus; for "as many as received," came to "him, to them gave he power to become the sons of God."

～∽

That You May Enter Heaven—Come

AS THERE IS A PLACE of punishment for the wicked, so there is a heaven of glory for all who come to Jesus. God, in his great love to sinners, sent his Son not only to deliver them from hell, but to make them happy and glorious with him forever. When a believer dies, though his body decays, his soul is at once with Jesus, which is "far better." How delightful is the description the Bible gives of heaven. We are told that sickness, sorrow, and death never enter there; that cares, fears, and anxieties are never felt there; that poverty, privation, unkindness, and disappointment are never known there. The body that will rise from the grave will be "incorruptible," and will never experience pain, weariness, or decay. Old age will never enfeeble, for there will be perpetual youth; and death will never snatch away those we love, for death itself will be destroyed. What is still better, there will be no more sin, but all hearts will be full of holy love to God, and to one another. Every one will rejoice in the society and happiness of every one else, and God himself will dwell among them. All the good men of former ages will be there—the martyrs, and apostles, and prophets.

There, too, we shall meet with angels and archangels; and more than all, we shall behold Jesus in his glorified human body—we shall see his face and ever be with the Lord. To show how glorious heaven is, it is compared to a city with streets of gold, gates of pearl, and walls of jasper and emerald; to a paradise with a river clear as crystal, and the tree of life with healing leaves; to a place of rest after labor; to a father's house, a happy home.

"They shall obtain joy and gladness, and sorrow and sighing shall flee away. Everlasting joy shall be upon their heads. In his presence is fullness of joy, and at his right hand are pleasures forevermore."

"The best joys of earth are soon gone. Riches fly, health decays, friends depart, death is written on all things." But the joys of heaven are forever, and forever, and forever. Reader, this heaven may be thine. Jesus keeps the door, but he has opened it wide for all sinners to enter. If you will not come to Jesus, you cannot enter heaven; for he is the door, the only door. But he invites you to come. Yes, however guilty and vile you are, heaven may, and certainly will be yours, if you come to Jesus. "To you is the word of this salvation sent." O, then, for heavenly bliss, come to Jesus.

※ ※

Who Is Jesus?

THIS IS A MOST important inquiry, because no one can rightly comply with the invitation, "Come to Jesus," without a correct knowledge of who he is. Much depends on the answer we give to the question, "What think ye of Christ?"

※ ※

Jesus Is God

BEFORE HE APPEARED on earth, he had from eternity possessed all the perfections of Deity. As the Father is God, so also Jesus is God. This is a great mystery, but it is a great truth. The Bible clearly declares it. He is called "The Word;" and St. John tells us,

> "In the beginning was the Word, and the Word was with God, and the Word was God. All things were made by him, and without him was not anything made that was made."

And "The Word was made flesh, and dwelt among us." Speaking of himself, Jesus said, "Before Abraham was, I am." He referred to the "glory which he had with the Father before the world began;" and declared, "I and the Father are one." We are told that he is "the brightness of the Father's glory," "the image of the invisible God," "God manifest in the flesh;" that "he is the same yesterday, today and for ever;" and that "in him dwelleth all the fulness of the Godhead bodily."

Jesus, therefore, is God; and is perfect in power and wisdom and goodness. There is nothing he cannot do; and as he never can change, he will never be unfaithful to his promises. Now, poor sinner, this is just such a Saviour as you want. If you needed a protector from some great danger you would go to some one who was mighty. Who so mighty as Jesus? All that God can do, he can do. There are no difficulties, dangers, or foes he is unable to conquer for you. Whatever your weakness, his strength must be all sufficient. It is not some frail fellow-man, it is not even an angel you are to trust in. It is one infinitely higher than all created beings—even the great God, mighty to save. We should have cause to fear, if any one inferior were our Saviour. But we may feel quite safe when he undertakes to save, who is the Lord of heaven and earth. Who can harm us, if he promises to help us? "If God be for us, who can be against us?" His power, wisdom, holiness, and goodness, are all employed on our behalf, as soon as we come to Jesus. With such a Saviour we cannot perish. "He is able to save to the UTTERMOST."

Jesus Is Man

THIS IS AS TRUE as that he is God. "God so loved the world that he sent his only begotten Son." And Jesus, though "equal with God,"

> "took upon him the form of a servant, and was made in the likeness of men, and was found in fashion as a man."

He was predicted as "a man of sorrows," and frequently styled himself "the Son of man." He became man in order to obey the law we had broken, and to suffer the punishment we had merited. Because no one can see God, he lived among us as a man, that from his spirit and conduct we might have a clearer idea of what God is. Thus he said "He that hath seen me, hath seen the Father." And he became a man that, suffering what we suffer, we might feel sure that he can sympathize with us. Thus we read, "In that he himself hath suffered, being tempted, he is able to succor them that are tempted;" and,

> "We have not a high-priest which cannot be touched with the feeling of our infirmities, but was in all points tempted like as we are."

Think, then, of Jesus as a man. Yonder is a funeral. It is a widow's only son, and she follows the corpse with a broken heart. Who is the man that sees her afar off, pities her, goes up to the dead body, restores it to life, and delivers the son to his mother? That loving but mighty man is Jesus. Who is this standing amid a crowd of little children, and taking them so kindly in his arms to bless them? It is Jesus. Who is that mourner weeping at the grave of Lazarus? It is Jesus. Who is it that all the sick, and the poor, and the sorrowful run after, and who heals and comforts them all, refusing none? It is Jesus. He is still the same; a loving, tender, compassionate man. You need not be afraid of him; he is a man, your brother. It is he who says to you, "Come unto me." Listen to him, sinner. He is the mighty God, and able to save you; but he is also the "man of sorrows," and full of sympathy and love. He knows, feels, and pities all your weakness and frailties and fears. He bids you not be afraid. As a brother-man, he stands with looks of unutterable kindness, and says, "come unto me, come unto me." O treat not with indifference so loving a Friend. Listen to him. Let your heart be touched by his tenderness. Trust in his promises. Come to Jesus at once. Rely on him as your Saviour, and obey him as your King, and he will be to you the "Friend that sticketh closer than a brother."

☙ ❧

He Is the Saviour of Sinners

"THIS IS A FAITHFUL saying, and worthy of all acceptation, that Jesus Christ came into the world to SAVE SINNERS"—"Him hath God exalted to be a Prince and a Saviour." This alone brought him to our wicked world. And how does he save? By standing in our place, and bearing the punishment we merited. We have broken the law, but he has perfectly kept it; for he was holy, harmless, undefiled, separate from sinners. We deserved death for our sins. "The soul that sinneth, it shall die." But he died for us. "He gave his life a ransom for many." We were under the curse. "Cursed is every one who continueth not in all things written in the book of the law to do them." But "he was made a curse for us." "He was wounded for our transgressions, he was bruised for our iniquities; and by his stripes we are healed." "He bare our sins in his own body on the tree." This is why he became a man, was "despised and rejected, a man of sorrows, and acquainted with grief." He "carried our sorrows." This is why he suffered temptation, groaned in Gethsemane, in his agony sweat great drops of blood, was scourged, spit upon, crowned with thorns, and nailed upon the cross. "He gave his life a ransom for many." We were slaves—he came to set us free. But the price he paid was his own blood. "Redeemed with the precious blood of Christ." We were prisoners at the bar, condemned to die; but he left his Father's throne, and came and stood at our side, saying, "I will die for them, that they may be forgiven and live for ever." And now that he has returned to his glory in heaven, he lives to save us. He watches over us, speaks to us by his word and by his Spirit, listens to our prayers, advocates our cause, helps us in our weakness, and "ever liveth to make intercession for us." He thus saves us both by his death and his life. He has paid all our debts, and is ready to supply all our wants. He saves those who trust in him from the sting of death, and delivers them from condemnation at the judgment day. We must appear before the Judge as guilty sinners; but if we can use this plea, "I trust in Jesus, who died for me," he will at once declare us to be fully acquitted, pardoned, saved. He says to thee, reader,

> **"Poor sinner, thou art in danger of hell; but I have brought thee a free pardon, purchased with my own blood. I died for thee. I am able to save thee. Come unto me."**

He Is the Only Saviour

JESUS SAID, "I AM THE WAY: no man cometh unto the Father but by *me*." We can only obtain pardon from God by coming to Jesus for it. All God's mercy for sinners has been placed in the hand of Christ, and no one can obtain it but from him. Some who neglect Jesus, yet hope in God's mercy. To them God But if they reject Jesus, they reject mercy. To them God will only be an angry Judge, "a consuming fire." Our own good works cannot save us. Our best actions are sinful; and if they were perfect, they could not atone for the past. St. Paul says, "By the works of the law shall no flesh living be justified." If we could have entered heaven by our own merits, why should Christ have died? We could have saved ourselves. O trust not in your own works, your good character, your honesty and charity—nothing but the righteousness and death of Jesus can save. Some think because they have been baptized and taken the sacrament, because they read their Bible, keep the Sabbath, and go to church they will be caved. Multitudes have done this, yet, having never come to Jesus, are now in hell. No sacrament, ceremony, creed, or church can save. None but Jesus can. Some rely on their priest. Sad mistake. Poor man, he needs a Saviour for himself. He cannot save his own soul, much less yours. None but Jesus can give absolution. His blood alone cleanseth from sin. Some pray to saints, angels, and the Virgin Mary; but who can tell whether they can listen to any who address them? and if they could can they save the soul? The Bible tells us plainly,

> **"There is one mediator between God and men, the man Christ Jesus."**

> **"Neither is there salvation in any other; for there is none other name under heaven given among men, whereby we must be saved."**

Look then to no one else. Trust only in Jesus. He is seated on a throne of mercy, and invites all poor sinners to come at once close up to him. He alone has pardon to give. Why then stop to talk to fellow sinners, or even angels, when no being can help you but Jesus? You need no one to introduce you to him. The beggar and the prince, the black man, and the white, the ignorant and the learned, those clothed in rags and those in silk attire, are equally welcome. All are invited. You sin by looking anywhere else for help. He says, "look unto me, and be ye saved, all ye ends of the earth." Look away from men, away from yourself; look only to Jesus, for he alone can save.

He Is A Loving Saviour

THERE COULD BE NO stronger proof of this than his coming from heaven to suffer and to die. His own words were "Greater love hath no man than this, that a man lay down his life for his friends." Why did he leave a holy heaven for a sinful world; the songs of angels for the temptations of devils, a throne of glory for a cross of agony? It was love only, only love. Love, not to friends but to foes. "While we were yet sinners, Christ died for us." He showed his tender love in a thousand ways when on earth, going about doing good, healing all manner of sickness, never turning from the poor and the sad, always the "Friend of sinners." How he wept over Jerusalem, as he thought of her sins and approaching sufferings. When in the agonies of death, how kindly he spoke to the penitent thief at his side; and how earnestly he prayed for his mocking murderers: "Father, forgive them; for they know not what they do." He might easily have called forth an army of angels to deliver him; but if he had not died, we could not have been saved: and therefore, because he loved us, he drank the bitter cup to its very dregs.

Now that he has risen again, his love to sinners is as great as ever. Love prompts him to intercede for us, to pity us, to send his Spirit to help us, to wait to be gracious, and saves us. He loves you; he died for you; he looks down with pity on you; he calls you to come to him. His love has spared you till now, though you have rejected him. His love bears with your sins, and again at this moment entreats you to accept a pardon purchased by his blood. If some friend had spent his fortune to deliver you from prison, or risked his life to save yours, could you treat him with neglect? But Jesus has done far more. He died to redeem you from eternal woe, and make you happy for ever in heaven. He comes to you, and showing the marks of his wounds, he says,

> **"See how I loved thee, sinner. I love thee still. Come unto me, that I may save thee from sin and from hell."**

O reject not so gracious a Saviour. Trample not under feet such wonderful love. You will never meet with such another Friend. Trust him. Love him. You will always find him full of pity and tenderness. He will comfort, guide, protect, and save you amid all the dangers and sorrows of life, deliver you from the sting of death, and then make you happy for ever in heaven. O come to this loving Saviour.

He Will Be Our Judge

"WE MUST ALL APPEAR before the judgment seat of Christ." The man of sorrows will come again as the God of glory, and "before him will be gathered all nations."

> "Behold, he cometh with clouds; and every eye shall see him, and they also who pierced him."

How encouraging to believers. He is the very person they would have chosen for themselves, and when they see him on the throne they will rejoice, for their best Friend, who has promised to save them, will be their Judge, and therefore they will feel secure. But how dreadful for those who have rejected him. How terrible his look of reproach to those who pierced him by their sinful neglect. How dreadful to hear the voice which now says, "Come unto me," say, "Depart, ye cursed."

Suppose a prisoner is soon to be tried for a crime for which he will lose his life. He is visited by a man of humble appearance, but great kindness, whose heart seems to overflow with pity for the prisoner. He has been laboring very hard for the culprit's escape at the trial. He tells him what he has done, and proves that he may be safely trusted. He assures him that he is quite able to secure his acquittal or his pardon, if only the prisoner is willing he should do so. He says,

> "I pray you let me come forward at the trial, and speak on your behalf. Let me plead your cause. I have saved many a prisoner whose case was as bad as yours; I can save you. I ask no payment. Love alone prompts me. Consent to let me help you."

But the prisoner is reading, talking, or sleeping, and takes no notice of this friend. He comes again and again; but the prisoner dislikes his visits, and by his actions asks him not to come and disturb him. The trial comes on. The prisoner is brought into court. He looks at the judge in his robes of office; and sees he is the despised friend who came to him in his cell. But now his countenance is solemn and his voice severe. He who was refused as a friend now appears only as a judge.

Sinner, he who as a judge will occupy the throne at the last day, comes to thee in thy prison, and offers to be thy Saviour. He is willing to plead thy cause, and promises thee a free and full deliverance at the trial. Refuse him not, for soon you must stand at his bar. Trust in him as your Advocate, if you would not tremble before him as your judge. Accept his invitation, if you would not hear him pronounce your doom. Welcome him now to your heart, that he may welcome you then to his kingdom.

Where Is Jesus?

IT WAS THE LANGUAGE of Job, "O that I knew where I might find him, that I might come even to his seat!" Is this thy language, poor sinner? Art thou anxious to know where to find Jesus? He is no longer on earth in human form, but has returned to heaven. There you may find him, seated on a throne of mercy, waiting to give eternal life to all who come to him. You may think it far to go, but the prayers of sinners reach heaven the very moment they are uttered, and are listened to by Jesus with kind attention. Yet if this seems hard to understand, know assuredly that Jesus is not only in heaven, but on earth too. He is God, and therefore is everywhere. He said to his disciples, "I am with you always." He is constantly present among us. In the sick chamber there is Jesus, ready to comfort the afflicted disciple who lies on that bed of pain. In the secret spot to which the sinner has retired to confess his sins, there is Jesus waiting to say, "Be of good cheer; thy sins are forgiven thee: go in peace." In the church or the room where many or few have assembled to praise and pray, there is Jesus waiting to supply their wants. "Wheresoever two or three are gathered together in my name, there am I in the midst of them."

Reader, he is near thee. Now, while thine eye reads this page, he stands close at thy side. He whispers in thine ear. He invites thee to seek him. If anxious to find him, thou hast no long journey to take, no long time to wait before thy request can reach his ear. He is nearer than the friend sitting beside thee, for he is at thy heart's door, knocking for entrance. Wherever thou goest he follows thee, his hands laden with blessings, which he offers to thee freely. He compasses thy path, and thy lying down; but it is always to do thee good. In the morning he stands at thy bedside, offering to clothe thee with his white robe of righteousness; and when thou art seated at the table, he asks thee to eat that bread of life which will save thy soul from death. He is so near that he will notice thy first faint effort to come to him, and will stretch out his hand to help thee. He is so near that he will see thy first tear of penitence, and catch thy first sigh for pardon. He is so near that before you call he will answer, and while you are yet speaking he will hear.

Sinner, where-ever you are, there is Jesus. So that in all countries, under all circumstances, by day and by night, at home and abroad you may come to Jesus.

What Is Meant by "Coming to Jesus?"

"MUCH IS SAID OF COMING to Jesus, but how can I come? He is in heaven, and how can I go there to speak to him? I am told he is also everywhere, but I cannot see him, and how can I go to him? If he were but on earth as he once was, there is no trouble I would not take. I would sell all I possess to pay for my journey; I would travel hundreds of miles. No difficulties should daunt me. I would set off at once. I would go to him and push my way through the crowd, as the sick used to do, in order to be healed. I would fall down before him, and lay hold of his garment, or embrace his feet; and I would say,

> **'Lord Jesus, save me. I came not to be healed of blindness or lameness, or leprosy, but of sin. My heart is diseased with iniquity. I am in danger of God's wrath, and of eternal damnation. Lord, save me, I perish.'**

But alas, Jesus is no longer among us, and I cannot understand what is meant by coming to him."

Dear reader, do all this in thy heart, and then you will come to Jesus. What do you think would be the advantage of going to him, and falling before him, and holding his garment, and speaking to him as the sick and the lame used to do? Would it not be to let him know your wants? These he knows already. Without all this trouble, you can make him understand that you wish him to save you. Think of him, let your heart feel respecting him, and let your cries ascend to him, just as if you saw him. Be as earnest as if there was a crowd round him which you wished to push through. Call to him as that blind man did, who, though he saw him not, cried out, "Jesus, thou son of David, have mercy on me!"

You are better off than they who lived when he dwelt on earth. They had often to journey far. They sometimes could not get near him for the press of people. But you may have him as much to yourself as if there were no other sinner that needed him. He is always near and within call; and though you cannot see him, he sees you, knows all you feel, and hears all you say. Coming to Jesus is the desire of the heart after him. It is to feel our sin and misery; to believe that he is able and willing to pardon, comfort, and save us; to ask him to help us, and to trust in him as our Friend. To have just the same feelings and desires as if he were visibly present, and we came and implored him to bless us, is to come to him, though we do not see his face nor hear his voice. Repenting sinner, your very desire for pardon, your prayer, "Jesus, save me"—this is coming to him.

Come by Prayer

THOUGH YOU CANNOT SEE Jesus, you can speak to him. You can pray. God has permitted, and even commanded us to do this. How great a privilege to be allowed to speak to God. "Call upon me in the day of trouble." "Watch and pray." "Pray without ceasing." Prayer requires no fine, well-arranged sentences. The simplest utterance of your heart's desire is prayer. Those desires, themselves, un-breathed, are prayer. You need not wait until you can enter a church to pray; you may pray everywhere.

And Jesus is always waiting for the prayers of poor sinners; so that not one ever escapes his notice. His ear is always open. It is difficult to speak to kings and princes: they can only be seen sometimes, and then only a few persons are permitted to come near them. But all may come with their petitions to Jesus, however poor and despised, and at all times too. Whatever good things you want for the soul, pray. For pardon, for a new heart, for faith, for holiness, for comfort, pray. You cannot pray in vain. You may be sure of such prayers being answered.

There are some things which even God cannot do. He cannot sin, and he cannot refuse to listen to a poor sinner's prayer, for he has promised. "Ask, and it shall be given you," said Jesus: and his word declares, "He cannot deny himself." Be then encouraged to pray. However vile and helpless you think you are, you are not too bad to pray. Pray, if you can only utter such a petition as this, "Save, Lord, or I perish!" Make a habit of prayer. Find some place where you can be alone. "When thou prayest, enter into the closet, and shut the door." Rise before the work of the day begins, that you may have time to pray. Lay open your heart before God. Tell him how vile, and helpless, and wretched you are. Confess your sins, and cry for pardon. Read the Bible, and ask for that holiness which is commended there. Say,

> "Lord, I am ignorant, teach me. My heart is hard, soften it. Convert me by thy Holy Spirit. Help me to come to Jesus—to believe, love, and obey him. Save me from sin, and fit me for heaven!"

And let your heart throughout the day often ascend to God, even while engaged in your necessary labor. "Pray without ceasing." If the answer does not seem to come at once, pray on, and success is certain. A praying soul *can never* be lost. You cannot perish while you are sincerely calling upon Jesus, saying, "Lord, have mercy upon me a sinner."

~ ~

Come In the Boldness of Prayer

IT IS WONDERFUL that creatures so sinful as we are, should be allowed to pray at all. When we consider what we are, and what God is, we may well tremble when we come to him, and fear lest he should reject us. But he has encouraged us to come, even with "boldness, to the throne of grace." This does not mean that we are to come without deep reverence and humility, but that we are to pray with a full persuasion that God will answer us. There are many examples of answers to prayer. Hezekiah prayed, and the army of Sennacherib was smitten with death. Elijah prayed, and fire came down to consume his sacrifice. The apostles prayed, and the Holy Ghost descended upon them with miraculous gifts. The church prayed, and Peter was delivered from prison by an angel. We are not to expect that all we ask for respecting this life will be given us, for we often desire what would do us harm. We may be sure, however, that God will give us what is best. But when we pray for blessings for our souls—for pardon, and holiness, and salvation--we may be quite certain of being answered; for we are told, that if we ask anything according to God's will, he heareth us; and we are also told, that God is "willing that all men should be saved." Jesus said, "Ask, and it shall be given;" and, "Whatsoever ye shall ask in my name, that will I do." He prays for us.

Our best prayers are far too unworthy for God to notice, but he listens because Jesus pleads. If you wrote a petition to a king, but none at the palace knew you, and you were dressed in rags, and after doing your best, the writing was covered with blots, would you not fear that you would never be admitted, or if you were, that the petition would not be read? But suppose the king's son were to come, and say, "I will present your petition myself, and ask my father to grant it." Jesus does this. He presents our feeble prayers, and says, "For my sake, bless this poor sinner, and grant his request." And we are told that "him the Father heareth always." "He ever liveth to make intercession."

Trembling, mourning sinner—rejoice. You have a friend at court. However unworthy your petitions are, Jesus prays for you, and his prayers always prevail. What more can you need to encourage you? Come then with

> "boldness to the throne of grace, that you may obtain mercy, and find grace to help in time of need."

Come In Faith

IN THE NEW TESTAMENT we read very much about faith. We are said to be "justified by faith," and "saved by faith," and are told to "believe in the Lord Jesus Christ, that we may be saved." Faith is confidence, reliance. If I am hungry, and a kind friend offers me something and says it is bread, but it is dark, and I cannot see, yet, if I begin at once to eat it, this is faith. I trust in his word. If I am sick, and medicine is given me which I am told will do me good, and I drink it, this is faith. I believe or have confidence in the doctor's skill. Jesus came into the world to die for sinners. He says,

"Believe in me. I have purchased a full pardon for you, and you may go free. It cost my own blood to obtain it, but you are freely welcome to it. If you will obey my words, and trust in my protection, I will engage to save you from death and hell: I am quite able to do this. Here is bread to eat, which will make you live for ever if you eat it; here is a medicine which will cure your soul's sickness that you shall never die. Come unto me—believe in me, and you shall be saved."

Faith is just trusting to what Jesus says. Faith is simply coming to Jesus. He has died for thee. Believe it, and take the benefit of his dying. He has opened the prison door for thee. Believe it, and make thine escape. He is willing to bear thy burden for thee. Believe it, and cast thy sins upon him. He has paid all thy debts. Rejoice. He brings salvation to thee, and says, "It shall be thine, if thou are willing." Stretch forth thy hand, take it with a grateful heart. Like the prodigal in the parable, thou hast wandered far from home; but Jesus has obtained for thee permission to return. Thy Father, for his sake, is willing to welcome thee back. Believe it, and say, "I will arise and go to my Father." You desire to be trusted by your husband, or wife, or children; you would feel hurt by their doubting your word. So Jesus wishes to be believed when he says, "Poor sinner, I am able and willing to save thee. Come unto me." Do not grieve him by distrusting his word. If you do not come because you think you are too great a sinner, you say, in effect, that he is not able to save you, though he tells us, "he is able to save to the uttermost ALL who come." You make him a liar. Believe that he really will do what he promises. Go to him at once. Say to him, "Lord, I believe; help thou mine unbelief. Thou art able to save to the uttermost—save me."

Come As A Sinner—Just As You Are

PERHAPS YOU SAY, "HOW can I, who am so vile a sinner, venture to come near the holy Jesus? Will he permit such a wretch to approach him? Must I not wait till I am more fit?" Dear fellow-sinner, your very sinfulness is your best fitness. What you think to be a hinderance is your best encouragement; for, "Jesus Christ came into the world to save sinners," and therefore to save such as you. "I came not to call the righteous, but sinners to repentance." Not that there are any who are really righteous, but there are many who think themselves so, and such persons will never be received by Christ.

We must come to him in our true character, if we come at all. We are great sinners. We have broken God's laws. We have indulged in wickedness in our hearts, as well as in open conduct; we have quenched the Spirit, and despised the love of Jesus. Everything we do is full of imperfection. We cannot make ourselves pure. And if we come to Jesus pretending we are righteous, we only mock him. Instead of thinking we are "rich, and increased in goods, and have need of nothing," we must come as those who are "poor, and miserable, and blind, and naked."

Thus we must come to Jesus, and confess our unworthiness. In one of his parables he spoke of a self-righteous man, who thanked God that he was better than others; and of a broken-hearted penitent, who did not venture to raise his eyes to heaven, but smote upon his breast, saying, "God be merciful to me a sinner!" It was the latter who went home pardoned and saved. And if we would be accepted by Jesus, we must go to him in the same spirit, saying, "God be merciful to me a sinner!"

And we must not wait, thinking that we shall ever be more worthy. No, our souls are stained through and through with sin, and all our washing will never get rid of one dark spot. The blood of Christ alone can make us clean. We can never make ourselves better. We must come to Jesus to make us better; and till then nothing is done. Our very first duty is to come to Jesus. Come then, poor sinner. Wait not another moment, foolishly thinking you will be more fit by and by. You will never be more fit, and never more welcome, than at this moment. Jesus knows, far better than even you do, how sinful and vile you are; yet he does not say, "Wait," but, rather, "Come." *Come*, then, with all your sins and weakness, and hardness of heart, come to Jesus. Come as a sinner, and come just as you are.

☙ ❧

"But I Am Not Worthy, and Cannot Come Aright."

IF YOU IMAGINE THAT any sinner is worthy of salvation, you quite mistake the nature of the gospel. It is a free gift, not a reward. No one is worthy. Paul, Peter, John were not worthy. But Jesus is so full of love that, unworthy as we all are, he invites us to come. If he makes our sin no objection, why should we? Jesus knows that filthy rags cover you, that a nauseous disease infects you; yet he says, "Come unto me." On account of these very things, he says, Come. How unreasonable, then, for you to refuse because you are unworthy?

You might as well say you were too hungry to eat, or too poor to receive help, as that you are too unworthy to come for pardon. Your very unworthiness makes you welcome. But you say you cannot come as you ought. Then come as you can. Jesus did not say, "Come unto me running or walking upright," but simply, "Come." Come in any manner, and you will be received. Come creeping, crawling—any way—only come. You say you do not repent enough. You never will; for penitence, like all other graces, is ever growing, and no one's penitence can equal his sins. But we are not saved because we repent enough, but, if we do repent at all, we are saved because Jesus died. You say you have not love enough. You never will have, till you get to heaven. But we are saved, not because we love God, but because he loves us.

You say you have not faith enough. True, and every Christian needs to pray, "Lord, increase my faith." But if you truly look to Jesus for salvation, this is faith; and though very weak, none who possess it can perish. But perhaps you say you heart is totally hard, and therefore that your mere cries of distress are not prayers which God can accept. Be encouraged by the case of Simon Magus. "His heart was not right in the sight of God;" he was "in the gall of bitterness, and in the bond of iniquity;" yet Peter said, "Pray God, if perhaps the thought of thy heart may be forgiven thee," which means, "If you indeed pray to God, your sins will be forgiven." Your condition cannot be worse than his; yet he was encouraged to come to Jesus. Come with a broken heart, he may heal it; or as Leighton says, "If thou find it unbroken, yet give it him, with a desire that it may be broken." However unable to come aright, make the effort: come as you can, only come; and Jesus will not, cannot reject you.

༄ ༄

"But I Fear I Am Not One of the Elect."

YOU HAVE NO CAUSE for this fear but your own fancy. Has God, or an angel, or the Bible told you so? Election, whatever it means, is God's work, not yours. Do not perplex yourself with his secret counsels, but attend to your own plain duties.

> "Secret things belong unto God; but those which are revealed belong unto us, that we may do all the words of this law."

We must leave the secret things, and attend to the revealed. Our duty is to do according to God's law. And this law is most clear. You are nowhere told you are not elect; but you are told that Jesus died for you, and you are invited to come to him. Vex your mind, then, no longer about such difficult subjects as election, but promptly obey what God commands. He says,

> "Cast away from you all your transgressions, and make you a new heart and a new spirit. Turn ye from your evil ways. Repent, and believe the gospel. Believe in the Lord Jesus Christ, and thou shalt be saved. Ask, and it shall be given you; seek, and ye shall find;

knock, and it shall be opened. Draw nigh to God, and he will draw nigh to you. Him that cometh unto me I will in no wise cast out."

Do what God says, and your salvation will be sure. Suppose you were very poor, and a rich man were to announce that he would give a pound to a hundred persons whose names no one knew but himself, but at the same time promised that he would give it to every one who applied for it; would you say, "I am afraid I am not among the favored number, therefore I will not ask for the money?" No; you would rather say, "Whether I am among the hundred or not, every one is invited, and therefore I will go." Do the same respecting eternal life. Do not sit still, teasing yourself with useless inquiries whether your name is in God's book.

Are you a sinner? "Oh yes." Well, then you are invited; for "Jesus came to save sinners," and "he is the propitiation for the sins of the whole world." The invitation is universal. "Whosoever will, let him take the water of life freely." Jesus said not, "Come unto me, ye whose names are in the book of life," but, "Come unto me, all ye that labor and are heavy laden."

Are you heavy laden with sin? Then come to Jesus and your salvation is certain. Come to Jesus, and then you may be sure your name will be found in the book of life. Come to Jesus, and you will be received as one of the elect; but if you stay away, you will perish.

"But I Have No Faith."

"I DO NOT FEEL my sins forgiven, and I am not sure I am saved. Many say they know the time when they found salvation, and that they have an inward witness that all is right with them. They have found peace; but I have not. I am full of doubts and fears, have no faith, and therefore fear Jesus will never receive me." My friend, you confound two things which greatly differ, faith and assurance. You have been speaking of assurance, not of faith. It is very delightful to feel sure of pardon and heaven; but it is quite possible not to feel this, and yet to possess faith. Faith is coming to Jesus as a poor sinner, and trusting to him alone for salvation. Assurance is feeling certain we are saved. They are quite different things. Faith is necessary for salvation, but assurance is not. Many people possess an assurance which is false, while they are destitute of faith; and many also have true faith, but do not enjoy assurance.

Suppose you were shipwrecked, and clinging to a part of the vessel over which the waves were furiously breaking. A life-boat comes out to you. It is so well built that it cannot possibly sink. The rowers are so skillful that they never failed to bring it safe to shore. They invite you to enter. You know that the vessel you cling to will soon be dashed to pieces. You believe the boat will take you safe to shore. You enter it. But when the huge waves toss it up and down, and seem about to overwhelm it, you are afraid, and perhaps do not lose your fear till you reach the shore. Getting into the boat was faith—being afraid while in it was the want of assurance. But though frightened, you were as safe as the rowers who had no fears. Your terrors did not endanger your safety, though it destroyed your peace. We are in a storm. Our sins have raised up the winds and waves of divine justice. The law thunders it curses against us. Hell yawns below.

Jesus is like the life-boat. He comes out to us and invites us to forsake all our own refuges, which are as frail as a sinking wreck, and to cast ourselves on him. Trusting in him alone is faith, though when you think of your sins and infirmities you may be full of doubts and fears, and often think you are not safe. Take encouragement then, trembling sinner. Do you feel yourself lost without Jesus; and is it your earnest prayer, "Save, Lord, or I perish?" Then, whatever your gloomy doubts, you do possess faith, saving faith—that faith of which Paul spoke when he said, "Believe in the Lord Jesus Christ, and thou shalt be saved." None can perish who thus come to Jesus.

Ye Who Are Young, Come

YOUTHFUL READER, BE PERSUADED to give your early years to God. There is a special promise for you: "Those that seek me early shall find me." Perhaps you think, "I am too young to be religious yet; let me enjoy the world a little; I have plenty of time before me." Too young to be religious? But you are not too young to sin, or too young to die, or too young to be cast into hell. You may not live to reach manhood, much less old age. Multitudes die as young as you. If you enter a burial-ground, how many of the graves are those of young people. Death may be even now preparing to strike you. Oh then come at once to Jesus. You greatly err, if you think religion will make you gloomy. It alone can render you truly happy.

Many young people have tried it, who will all tell you that the pleasures of piety are far better than all the delights of sin and vanity. You will find that this is true, if you come to Jesus. It is likely he will let his followers be less happy than the servants of the world? Besides, how can you dare to live a day longer rejecting him?

He commands us at once to believe and obey him. Every day we put off repentance we commit a fresh act of rebellion, and treasure up wrath against the day of wrath. You say you will repent when you are old. But we need the Spirit of God to help us to repent; and if you say, "While I am young I will serve Satan, and not till I am near death will I turn to God," do you think God will give you his Holy Spirit at all? Is not this to quench the Spirit? May you not become quite careless, and indisposed to repent? Very few are converted when old. If you come not to Jesus when you are young, it is not likely you will come at all. Habit will fasten strong chains around you, which will be harder to burst asunder every day. While you wait, Satan works. He is busy tying knots. You are his prisoner; and he is making the cords which bind you more and more secure. Whenever you sin he ties another knot. Every impression you smother, every hour you delay, adds a fresh knot. If you do not escape now, how can you expect to break loose when you are weaker, and your fetters stronger?

Oh then, "Remember now thy Creator in the days of thy youth." Come at once to Jesus, if you wish to come at all. He will be your guide amid the snares, your comfort amid the sorrows, your guardian amid the dangers of life. Lose not for one day the privilege of possessing such a friend. Say from this moment, "My Father, thou art the guide of my youth."

☙ ❧

Ye Who Are Advancing In Years, and Ye Who Are Aged, Come

WITH YOU THE MORNING of life is over. You have reached the mountain top, or are traveling down the valley on the other side. You are rapidly drawing nearer the tomb. Perhaps you are still busily occupied in the necessary labors of life; or inclination and the love of gain may involve you in many engrossing cares. But forget not the "one thing needful." We can do without any thing else, even life itself; but we cannot do without Jesus. The salvation of the soul is the one thing needful. You have been busy for many years in the concerns of this life, but as yet have found no time for religion. Your chief business is not even begun. But what trifles are all things else in comparison. In a few years it will be of no consequence whether we were rich or poor; but it will be of infinite consequence whether we come to Jesus or not. Multitudes have died around you. Neighbors and friends, many with whom you were at school, or started in life, are in their graves. You have been spared. But you might have been cut down as a barren tree—unprepared. God's forbearance may be almost spent. Soon the sentence may be pronounced, "Cut it down; why cumbereth it the ground?"

Perhaps you are advanced in years. My aged friend, how many solemn warnings did you prepare. Your wrinkled features, whitening hair, decaying strength, loudly tell you that the end is near. You are tottering on the edge of the grave. The young may live many years, but you cannot. Soon, very soon, you must die. Oh, how dreadful to stand before the judgment-seat of Christ, and give an account of a long life spent in rejecting him—of thousands of Sabbaths and sermons and privileges neglected.

O then come to Jesus now. Lose not a moment. You have not one to spare. You have indeed hardened your heart, and made repentance more difficult by neglecting religion so long; but if you earnestly implore the help of God's Holy Spirit, he will grant your petition even now. It is not too late. Though you have so long refused to listen to him, Jesus has not ceased to speak to you. Still he says, "Come unto me." He loves you still. He is waiting to save you still. Oh, trifle with him no longer. Look back. Death comes striding after you with rapid steps; he is very near. Judgment is close behind, and hell follows. They are on the point of seizing you. Flee this moment to Christ. Come to Jesus. He alone can save.

∽ ∾

Backslider, Come

YOURS IS A PECULIAR CASE; for you have already come to Jesus, but have wandered from him. You have been near, but now you are afar off. Your sin is very great. You have experienced something of the love of Christ, yet have forsaken him. You have enjoyed clearer light and greater advantages than those who have never known what religion is. You have been admitted within the fold, and tasted the sweet pasture with which the good Shepherd feeds his flock, yet you have strayed from the sacred enclosure. Your declension began perhaps in secret, by restraining prayer, and neglecting God's word. Or you yielded to some temptation, but did not go to Christ for pardon, and so you became gradually careless. You may still maintain an outward profession of piety, but your heart is not right in the sight of God. Perhaps you have plunged into worldly dissipations, and are an example of the saying, "If any man love the world, the love of the Father is not in him." Perhaps even worse, you have fallen into open sin, and brought public disgrace on the name of Christian. You have lost all those opportunities of doing good which, had you not been a backslider, you would have improved. Thus you have robbed God. You have discouraged other professors by your coldness and inconsistency, and been a hindrance to many who were inquiring,

"What must I do to be saved?"

Instead of being a blessing to others, you have been a curse. And what is more you have grieved the Holy Spirit, have crucified the Son of God afresh, and put him to an open shame. Yet Jesus, the kind Shepherd whose fold you have left, is willing to welcome you back. He seeks the sheep that have gone astray. He says,

> "O Israel return unto the Lord thy God. Say unto him, Take away all iniquity, and receive us graciously. I will heal their backslidings, I will love them freely; for mine anger is turned away. Return, ye backsliding children, and I will heal your backsliding, for I am merciful. Only acknowledge thine iniquity, that thou hast transgressed against the Lord thy God. Turn, O backsliding children, saith the Lord!"

Consider these kind words. Ponder well the parable of the prodigal son. What greater encouragement can you need? Though you have wandered from Jesus, you may come to him again. He is as willing to receive you as at first. Stop, then, in your backward career. Return unto the Lord; for "why will ye die?"

༄ ༅

Despairing Sinner, Come

PERHAPS YOU SAY, "THE MERCY of God is for others, not for me. I have been too vile. I have abused the greatest privileges, and stifled the strongest convictions. I have fought against God, and committed crimes I shudder to think of. There can be no pardon for me." Listen, sinner: God says, "Though your sins be as scarlet, they shall be white as snow." "As I live, I have no pleasure in the death of the wicked, but that he turn and live. Turn ye, turn ye: for why will ye die?" Listen, sinner: "The blood of Jesus Christ cleanseth us from all sin." ALL sin, and therefore yours.

Listen: "He is able to save to the uttermost ALL who come unto God by him." And therefore YOU.

Listen: "Jesus Christ came into the world to save sinners, of whom I am CHIEF." He saves the chief of sinners, and therefore can save you. David, who had committed murder—Peter, who denied him—the thief on the cross—thousands who cried, "Crucify him"—Paul the persecutor—were all saved. And He who saved them is able to save you.

Do you fear you have committed the unpardonable sin? Your anxiety is a sure proof you have not committed it. Whatever that sin is, it is certain that if any one were to commit it, he would never feel any true penitence for it. For the Bible in every page tells us, that all who repent shall be forgiven, that all who seek mercy shall find it; and Jesus says, "Him that cometh unto me I will in no wise cast out," that is, on no account whatever. So that we may be quite sure that no penitent sinner who comes to Jesus for pardon, has committed sins which cannot be forgiven. God is bound by his promise and oath to "abundantly pardon" every sinner who comes to Jesus for salvation; but still you may say, "I am a lost sinner." A brother of the celebrated Whitefield was at tea with Lady Huntington, who endeavored to cheer his despairing soul by speaking of the infinite mercy of Christ. "My lady," said he, "it is true; I see it clearly: but there is no mercy for me; I am a wretch entirely lost." "I am glad to hear it, glad at my heart that you are a lost man," was her reply. "What, my lady; glad that I am a lost man?" "Yes, Mr. Whitefield, truly glad, for Jesus Christ came into the world to save the lost." That word cheered his soul. He believed in Jesus, and soon after died in peace.

Sinner, rejoice; Jesus came to save the lost—to save thee.

⁂

Careless Sinner, Come

WHAT, A REBEL AGAINST GOD—hastening now towards death—doomed to hell, yet careless? Reader, are you one of those who are so busy with the trifles of this world as to pay no attention to the eternal realities of the next? Listen to the startling question of Jesus. Ponder it.

> **"What shall it profit a man, if he gain the whole world, and lose his own soul?"**

Suppose you saw a crowd walking along a meadow, at the end of which was a terrific precipice. They pass on merrily, plucking flowers, till, as they reach the edge, one after another falls over, and is dashed to pieces. Would you not call to them,

> **"Stop, stop! as you value your lives, turn back?"**

You are strolling onwards to a far more terrible fate. Yawning beneath you is the lake of fire—and do you still go forward?

Jesus calls to you, "Turn ye, turn ye; why will ye die?" But you see not the danger. You feel happy, and hope it will be all right with you hereafter. Have you never seen how smooth the stream is just before it leaps down the cataract? Such is your peace, soon to be broken by a fatal plunge into endless woe.

Many poisons are pleasant to the taste, and soothe those who drink into sweet slumbers, but from these slumbers they never awake. You are quaffing Satan's cup of death. What you think pleasant drink is deadly poison; and your unconcern about religion is the sign how dreadfully it is operating on your soul. Beware, lest you wake up in the flames of hell. Before it is too late shake off this lethargy. Your house is on fire; the roof will soon fall in and crush you. But you sit at ease, amused with trifles, and neglecting every warning. Many cry "fire, fire—fly for your life." But you pay no attention to the alarm. Jesus offers himself as a refuge, but in vain. Yet, though you regard it not, you are in danger. In danger you draw every breath. Danger is your traveling companion when you journey, and danger haunts your home. Danger hovers over you during the bustle of the day, and danger peeps between your curtains amid the silence of night. You may be prosperous, beloved, flattered, and thoughtless; but you are in danger. You may drown reflection in business, or by plunging deeper and deeper into worldly dissipation and sin; but you are in danger—in danger of wrath, death, hell. Oh flee to Jesus. There only we are safe. Escape by the door of salvation, while it is yet open; for it will soon be shut, and then you will knock in vain.

୧ ୨

Come Now: It Will Be Harder Work Tomorrow

PERHAPS YOU THINK IT WILL be as easy to repent at any future time as to-day. This is a most dangerous delusion. Impressions of all kinds wear away by repetition, unless they are made permanent by being acted upon. If you ever lived near a noisy mill, a roaring river, or the sea, you have found that the sound, which at first disturbed you, was afterwards scarcely noticed. Just so the truths of religion may deeply impress the mind; but if those impressions are not cherished, by acting in accordance with them, those truths will effect the mind less and less, till they are heard with total indifference. Jesus says, "Behold, I stand at the door and knock." He knocks by sermons, books, conversations, conscience, solemn warnings. The sound startles you; but if you do not rise and open the door, it will startle you less to-morrow, till at length you will not hear it at all. How many who once felt deeply about religion, now feel nothing, and are quickly and quietly traveling down to hell.

On the narrow ledges of the steep cliffs of the Yorkshire coast multitudes of sea fowl lay their eggs, by gathering which, some persons obtain a perilous livelihood. It once happened that a man, having fixed in the ground his iron bar, and having lowered himself down by the rope which was fastened to it, found, that, in consequence of the edge of the cliff bending over the part below, he could not reach the narrow ledge where the eggs were deposited, without swinging himself backwards and forwards. By this means he at last placed his foot on the rock, but in so doing lost his hold of the rope. His situation was most dreadful. The sea roared hundreds of feet below. It was impossible to climb either up or down. He must soon perish from want, or fall, and be dashed to pieces on the rocks. The rope was his only way of escape. It was still swinging to and fro; but when it settled it would be out of reach. Every time it approached him it was farther off than before. Every moment he waited his danger increased. He made up his mind. The next time the rope swung towards him he sprang forward, seized it, and reached the top in safety.

Sinner, your salvation is farther off every moment you wait. Hell is below. Death will soon cast you down. But Jesus is near to save you. He invites you to lay hold on him. It is your only hope. Grasp him by faith. You cannot miss your hold. He will bold you and draw you up to heaven. But the difficulty and danger are greater every moment you delay. Come to Jesus now.

∽ ∾

Come Now: Tomorrow May Be Too Late

YOU HAVE PERHAPS DECIDED to come to Jesus, but not just now. Like Felix, you say, "Go thy way for this time; when I have a convenient season, I will call for thee." Satan knows that if you put religion off, he is likely to keep you captive for ever. God says, "TODAY if you will hear my voice, harden not your hearts: behold NOW is the day of salvation." Satan whispers, "not today, but, tomorrow." He promises you shall give to God all your future days, if only he can secure for himself the present.

Oh, beware of tomorrow. Souls are generally lost, not because they resolve never to repent, but because they defer it till some future time, and still defer it till it is too late. Tomorrows have crowded hell. Perhaps you think you will wait till disease assails you. But a sick bed is the very worst place for repenting. Your mind may be so distracted by delirium, fever, or pain, or may so share in the weakness of the body, as to be unable to think. The peace in which multitudes seem to die is only the apathy of disease. Many, who, when ill, have professed to repent, on recovery have become more careless than before. It was not true conversion; and had they died they would have been lost. There is little hope of salvation in sickness. But such a season may never come. You may die without a moment's warning. Though in health today, you may be dead tomorrow.

And are you, when life is so uncertain, putting off salvation? A prisoner is under sentence of death. He knows not the fatal hour, but is told, that if before it strikes he petitions the governor, his life will be spared. He says, "I'll send tomorrow." And when tomorrow comes again, "Oh, there's time enough yet; I'll wait a little longer." Suddenly his door opens, and—behold the sheriff and the executor! "Oh, wait, and I'll write the petition." "No," they say, "the clock has struck—it's too late; you must die."

Poor sinner, you are condemned. You know not when you may die. It may be this very day. You put off repentance till tomorrow; but tomorrow you may be in hell. Christ knocks today; but remember death may knock tomorrow. Though you keep your best Friend outside, death will burst in, and hurry you away to the judge. Come to Jesus today. He is willing to save today. Heaven's gate is open today. Tomorrow may be too late.

❦

You Must Perish If You Do Not Come

"WHAT MUST I DO be saved?" "Believe in the Lord Jesus Christ." "What must I do to be lost?" "Neglect so great salvation." It is not necessary to do any thing. We are lost already. Jesus offers to save us; but if we reject his offer, we remain as we are. If a man were bitten by a deadly serpent, but refused to apply the only remedy, he must die. The gospel is the only cure for the soul; and if we neglect it, sin kills us. You need not be a thief or a murderer to lose your soul. You may conform to all the outward ordinances of religion, but if you come not to Jesus, you are lost.

Consider the solemn words, "How shall we escape, if we NEGLECT so great salvation?" Escape is impossible, if we neglect the only means of safety. A boat is drawn by the current of the river near to the foaming cataract, where it must perish; but there is one solitary projecting rock near which it passes, where some men are waiting with a rope. Suppose the crew neglect to catch it—how can they escape? Neglect is their ruin.

Jesus alone can save the soul.

> "Neither is there salvation in any other; for there is none other name under heaven given among men, whereby we must be saved."

Oh, sinner, your damnation is sure, if you reject Jesus. And how great will be your guilt and punishment! There remaineth no more sacrifice for sins, but a certain fearful looking for of judgment and fiery indignation, which shall devour the adversaries.

> "He that despised Moses' law died without mercy; of how much sore punishment shalt he be thought worthy who hath trodden under foot the Son of God, and hath done despite unto the Spirit of Grace?"

What delusion has seized thee? Dost thou think God will not execute his threatenings, that thou will escape his piercing eye, or the rocks will cover thee? Vain hopes. There is no escape but by coming to Jesus, and simple neglect is certain perdition.

> "Because I called, but ye refused, I also will laugh at your calamity, I will mock when your fear cometh. Then shall they call, but I will not answer; they shall seek me, but shall not find me; for they did not chose the fear of the Lord, and despised all my reproof."

O sinner, escape this awful threatening. Jesus now stands with open arms. He entreats you to come and be saved. Refuse his grace no longer. Come with all your sins and sorrows—come just as you are—come at once. He will in no wise cast you out. Come to Jesus. *Come to Jesus.*

I WILL COME TO JESUS

Just as I am, without one plea,
   But that thy blood was shed for me.
And that thou bidst me come to thee,
   O Lamb of God, I come!

Just as I am, and waiting not,
   To rid my soul of one dark blot—
To thee whose blood can cleanse each spot.
   O Lamb of God, I come!

Just as I am—poor, wretched blind—
   Sight, riches, healing of the mind,
Yes, all I need, in thee to find,

O Lamb of God, I come!

Just as I am—though tossed about;
    With many a conflict, many a doubt,
With fears within, and foes without,
    O lamb of God, I come!

Printed in Great Britain
by Amazon